WHATEVER YOU
MAY SAY

WHATEVER YOU MAY SAY

POEMS

KURT HEINZELMAN

PINYON PUBLISHING

Montrose, Colorado

Cover Art "Horse In Stone" by Steve Friebert

Photograph of Kurt Heinzelman by Eric Beggs

Design by Susan Entsminger

First Edition: August 2017

Pinyon Publishing
23847 V66 Trail, Montrose, CO 81403
www.pinyon-publishing.com

Library of Congress Control Number: 2017947520
ISBN: 978-1-936671-44-1

ACKNOWLEDGMENTS

Some of these poems were first published elsewhere, and I am grateful to their publishers:

"Elevations: A Photoessay" in *Pinyon Review*

Selections from "Lone Star Haiku" in *Borderlands: Texas Poetry Review*

"Water" in *Texas Weather*, eds. Terry Dalrymple and Laurence Musgrove

"Still Life" in *Improbable Worlds*, ed. Martha Serpas

"Heine: 'Early One Morning'" in *Translation*

"Skyscrapers by the Sea," "Ecclesiastical Sonnet," and "Early Morning Canso" in *Bridge Magazine*

"Stopping by Words" under the title "Stopping by Words: A Monologue" was selected in an open national competition and performed by Bellingham Repertory Dance Company in conjunction with Chuckanut Sandstone Writers Theater, Firehouse Performing Arts Center, Bellingham, Washington, choreographed by Pam Kuntz, Angela Kiser, and Ella Mahler, first performed by Pam Kuntz, April 2008. The performance was reprised in *The Best of Phrasings - In Word and Dance* Festival, Fifth Anniversary, 2013.

"The Warmth of Winter" in *North American Review*

"Winkelmann, Texas" in *Texas Poetry Calendar 2013*

Several poems included here were first published in the collections *The Halfway Tree* and *Black Butterflies*, both printed by Randolph Bertin.

Many thanks to my fellow enthusiasts, Louise, Steve, Philip, Sue, Lucia, Paul, Jane, John, Betty Sue, Bill, Mary, Robin, and Amanda—you are a "godly company," as Chaucer says, for "felawship" and cheer.

Thanks to Ken Fontenot and Arwyn Groeneveld for help with the German; and to Max Porter and Matt Valentine for helping me find a title.

For Sue, as always

CONTENTS

3.

4.

5.

The poem is
Always
Each time

The first adventure,
The last, the only,

Where all is
In play, all
Is displayed.

—Guillevic

1.

ELEVATIONS: A PHOTOESSAY

Sometime at the first light
or in the darkness before it
before there is no way out
but to fling yourself
headlong towards it

the shutter of distance
flashes
a focus develops
tools
lie webbed in your hands

the peak leaves
its sliver of light
under cloud cuticles
over its rim the moon sets
like the moisture on plants

in the gloom the ropes
are gathered
coiled and knotted
a tight pack
and lines are put out

/

ear
lend me your cheer

heart
happen regularly

eye
travel farther

from me
than what is clear

feet
take a stand

if this is it
voice

do what you will

/

mounted on the pin
of dawn

a red hawk
enters the sky

its white ships
like dice

its collection
of blue hats

the croupier
of winds

as the peak
rises at you

like a bought boxer
with money to burn

/

I'm standing where
you can't see

the parquet of riprap
lichen enseaming

what's underfoot
what takes root

at each step
each slip

of the light
each slide's click

/

Night falls and you
repeat to the dark
what you expected
would slip from you always

shedding its light like a church

Night falls and you
repeat to yourself
whatever passed laughing
reading the wind's empty palms

trailing its light like a coast

/

The ax handles you find
mangled in circles of fir
stripped of the salt of their hands

The rest of the day you spend
sweating out what can never be
wholly refused

The next morning you walk out
and the next and the next
sleeker than any reticence

And you don't stop walking
because it is almost like dying
this reticence

I

Cold it is not cold here it is colder
rappelling off the rock face you hear
yourself humming to yourself lines
drawn taut as water plaiting down
the whole pulsing length of you
and of air and of where you are found
fixed by hooks across the flat
cliffs sway and the pull and the spray
and the crystal spin of your breath
sending and receiving messages

BODIES FALLEN IN
FIELDS OF SUNFLOWERS

*In Memoriam: Malaysia Airlines Flight 17
shot down over the Ukraine by Russian-backed
separatists. For weeks access was denied to the
site of the wreckage in fields of sunflowers.*

Once in full bloom
their faces stop turning
to follow the sun

Their stems are rough and hairy
but their flowers daisy-like
for really they are

members of the aster family
like those reddish ones
there in that white bowl

Three millennia before Christ
America's native peoples
cultivated these flowers of the sun

they thought more important even than corn
Their Spanish conquerors brought
the seeds home to Europe

In the nineteenth century the Czar's
botanists hybridized the commercially
viable "Mammoth Russian Sunflower"

principally for its oil
judged acceptable
by the Orthodox at Lent

Returned to the New World
near the beginning
of the "American Century"

the plants were used as silage for hogs
before their full uses
were discovered anew

Driving near Gratiot,
Wisconsin, I passed by
field after field of them

sown in that sober
four-square prairie
way so that the road

turning always at right
angles left you unable
to see over or around them

My father, riding shotgun
beside me, told of our family,
how they came from a village

in the Kingdom of Württemberg,
neither of which exists
any longer, so many wars later

Having escaped the Prussian
conscription of their sons
they were hoping to land

where bodies could stand
tall as sunflowers
under spacious skies

amid amber waves of grain

EARLY MORNING CANSO

Blue [is] the light that gets lost.
—Rebecca Solnit

Awake now,
      I'm watching that dog
            barking through the blinds

a strobe-light effect
      like Emily's dashes
            but in sonics

Fritillaries mingle
      amid passionflowers,
            hummingbirds

anticipate the unfolding salvia
      Here are the oscillations
            between a wanting

that is peculiar to the hour
      and what is attainable
            only

when all that's blue
      calves like ice
            into deeper blue

HORACE: "WHAT REMAINS"

after Odes 4.7

Run-off snow is prodigal bequeathing a meadow
        returned to grass.
Swollen a moment before the rivers now
        abide by their banks
though the chains of the earth have been shaken.
        Thaw follows frost
and spring turns on its heel becoming summer,
        while summer shifts
from foot to foot the blast of autumn's brilliance
        stiffens in winter's joints.
The earth, you see, moves as a woman moves
        naked in the company
of women. At evening it will have dawned on us
        that it was afternoon
all day. Old moons will open wounds
        new moons have healed
but once we have joined Tullus, Ancus, Aeneas
        and the rest
even these ludic tropes will be dust. ...
        How long we have got
we can only say: *than what we want*
        a little more,
a little less. When you see Minos, my friend,
        stepping from the shadows
to mark you for his own, the bottom line is
        yourself alone—
not what you've done nor hoped to pass on.

Remember Hippolytus
who, though chaste, was tossed beyond even
                Diana's outstretched arms.
Remember Pirithöus, would-be savior of Persephone,
                whom Hades rewarded
for his labors with a throne of adamantine
                chains, and Theseus,
too, remember, who vainly tried to save him,
                his mule-hearted friend.

GROUND WARS

Fresh on the heels of another wound-red
sunset gone hydrogen-peroxide frothy,
our friend Albert came striding from
Chicago barefoot across the manicured
grounds of Immaculate Heart, a few shafts
of moonlight taut as a brown trout hooked
or a dowser's wand biting the dirt.

He wore his torn "Creative Rotting" T-shirt
open to the heart, his pockets stuffed
with plastic, Thumbelina-size Disney Ducks,
when he was stopped by the cops and frisked.
Call it trespassing, call it bad luck, but men
who sport badges in this ventricle of Texas
want to see some photo ID or at least
some shoes, god damn it, and so they booked
him where he stood, the blades of St. Augustine
grass sprouting beneath his foot-soles, the lariat
of a good word twirling in heat waves of air.

When they pressed his fingers into ink
he listened to the far off, up-and-down
sluicing of the long Gulf coast of night.
Released on his own recognizance,
he watched from underneath the I-road
the length of MLK bleed beads of red
where bat-quick headlights pass across
our hard-edge Texas nightlife like stars.

VISITING THE SOMME

I must go over the ground again.
                    —Edmund Blunden, *Undertones of War*

Seven days of bombardment—
from artillery only, not the aerial
ways we do it now—laid more
ordnance than in all human
history up to that point, though
"that point" is as antiquated now
as a shilling or talent,
Deutschmark or franc.

Measure being temporal,
on the eighth day, which was
in fact the tenth—for, owing to
bad weather, two bombing days
were lost (like the planned
walkover, even time at that time
turned into a death march)—there
occurred the greatest loss
of military personnel
in a single day of warfare,
ever.

La forte somme—their
top price—you wonder, researching
what is *de bon marché*
in the *marché*. And the Somme
today?—on the map it's
straight but slow and old
and green when traced by foot,

not taking a *somme*, a nap,
but lazing through market
and village no older than
market and village in,
say, Newfoundland. Over here
les arbres d'alignement are
horse chestnuts now, perhaps
second-growth, with dense morel-
shaped leafage, along with a few
mountain ash, dotted with holiday-
jolly, red, inedible fruit among
roadside stands of *pêches*
jaunes (not yellow sins
péchés but white peaches)
all the way to the neatly
boxed cemeteries of white
chocolate wafers arrayed
upright like a luncheon treat
served on a trencher.

    Tout fait somme,
everything counts, as Siegfried
Sassoon, the "line-master" who
went "over the top" more often
than any other, told Wilfred Owen
as he lay not dying once more
in Craiglockhart:
               "*Rhythm*
is literally zigzaggedness,
not like water flowing but like
flow impeded, water over stones.
So rhythm undercuts meter

but offsets rhyme. Which is why,
old sport, we turned a good old
English word like *rime* to *rhyme*
so as to 'rhyme' with *rhythm*
which is Greek not English.

Gallipolli. It's Gallipolli
all over."

    "I have not been
at the Front," Owen wrote his mother,
"I have been in front of it."

    And now it's impossible
to find level ground anywhere
you walk on this battlefield,
to go out on even such a blue
midsummer noon as this one
—as blue as that one—
without losing your feet,
without mis-stepping,
though fences keep you
from entering fields of
ordnance still unexploded. …

    Somme toute. Let's say
it means "when all is said
and done." It hits you only
as you leave a small town
like this in France
and the road sign draws
a red line through
its name.

THE HALFWAY TREE

Sunday afternoon, and we going to visit
      the Halfway Tree.
It's just my father, a 9-year-old (a daughter
      mine, from this

marriage that still seems new to me), and me.
      Lost at the wheel,
I hear the youngest among us wondering out loud
      what a halfway

tree is halfway between. "Is it only half a tree?"
      The one who can
at 88 still name all the farms along these roads
      according to who's

owned them and since when, turns, beams, and tells
      how native runners—
Sauk or Potawatomi—paced out the trail between
      the Mississippi

and Lake Michigan and at the midpoint blazed
      this tree—and then,
in 1832, the first American Geologic Survey
      measured it

exactly so—within a yard, a nearly antiquated
      measure now
as feet like these we sometimes write in are.
      We find the place

at last by turning right on Halfway Tree Road,
        clearly marked.
Once at the tree another sign, its arrows pointing,
        makes us sure.

An orange snow-fence encircles the base.
        It seems a gnarled
ordinarily old burr oak that doesn't quite
        stand out enough

from half-a-dozen nearby maples of nearly equal girth.
        Frankly, we're let down.
The 9-year-old: "Why did they pick this tree out?"
        She's right: were those

old scouts so exact of measure? Or did some inner
        prudence doubt
a maple's inner strength? "Everything's grown up
        so all around"

(arrives the beamish voice). The driver,
        a man of learning,
adds, "You look at English landscapes as Kent
        and Capability

designed them, but now you can't see
        the picturesque
for the trees which have grown up in 200 years,
        with rhododendrons,

those fruits of Empire, shouldering out
            even the trees.
History may lose out to Time." Across the street
            ranch houses

with their prefab sheds approach in rows,
            their house numbers
stenciled on newly curbed streets in front of
            miles of yard.

On this side, though, where we are, there is
            a weathered corral
unseen before, and in the middle of it is a chestnut,
            grazing, hooded,

and a half-dozen mottled Indian ponies like ghosts
            of buffalo fanning
out across these Sugar River bottom lands
            or like mastodons

before retreating ice floes. We look at each other
            before driving off,
something like the force of horses turning us past
            the signposts

left for us down the soughing of our roads.

2.

LONE STAR HAIKU

Downdraft of pollen,
uplift of bat wings—
Asakusa? No, Austin.

A bruised peach—
moon caught in the twists
of flowerless wisteria.

Boy in the piney woods
sneezing, charred trunks
everywhere.

Oil donkeys pump
a stubble field
    sandhill cranes are grazing.

ENCHANTED ROCK

Asleep on my own right hand:
something winging above
    the bare dome.

Horizon: clouds swirling.
Down here: leaf storm.
    Adios, Stetson!

LLANO ESTACADO

Tumbleweed
stumbling over
tumbledown stones.

Haiku are small
like you, o curled
dachshund.

No bridge
the sun near setting
the arroyo surging.

—*after Buson*

Marathon   Paris
Alpine   Round Top
Mountain Home

A fall river
not fast enough
to float even a leaf.

FULTON BEACH

The faster the dachshund's legs
the longer the heron's stride
into flight.

Nopalitos grilling
no oil, no salt. No tequila?
No way, amigo.

Boerne   Bandera
Seguin   Sugarland
Flower Mound   Gruene

A cluster of owl pellets
nestled in locoweed,
broom.

Redwings in the bulrushes
sound like a downpour:
    not a drop on us.

Hail, haiku, deer:
we salute all y'all's
    singular plurality.

EMILY DICKINSON
IN THE HILL COUNTRY

Roadrunners—skip
Armadillos—hop
    Jackrabbits—cower.

Corpus Christi   Humble
Chappell Hill   Dime Box
    Dripping Springs   Snook

BEE CAVE

No bees hum here—
only Galleria neon,
    microwave towers.

A horseman riding home
to Utopia in the snow
    never rides alone.

The hole in the deck chair
softball-size:
    Water turned to stone.

Hailstones and peonies:
always the size
    of something else.

        —*In Memoriam*: George Carlin

Little wren below my window,
if you were dog-size
    you'd be deafening.

He's raking moldy leaves
into the colors of autumn,
    umbrellaed by butterflies.

Caesura this
unseasonable December,
    Haiku Guy!

The bells of Iglesia Pentecostes
fading, peach scent
    rings evening in.

    —*after Basho*

Windows down
Good breeze   No AC
Windows up
Hatch peppers roasting.

CHILDHOOD

She's in her car-seat batting
cobwebs of sunlight
that stick to her face

only to cry when we
turn a corner
and they're gone

That spiky fragrance of cholla.
Hola! —sun's out,
a mountain path.

How is it they stay
nineteen forever
these honky-tonk angels?

YELLOW FEVER CEMETERY

Dead a century ago,
their names lost in pockmarked stone.
Mosquitoes swarm
a new white stone's name.

Up here, papyrus,
pampas over there,
both unloppable.

In a high prairie corner
of tumbled homesteads
laurel by the fistful.

HILL COUNTRY

Country of hard scrabble,
scrub brush—outcrop
chafed by drouth

Landscape
like an angry throat
hurting for milk

Woman with no man
ridgeline like a scalded
ant mound

Flat-bellied earth
music for brasses:
sheriff-faced.

—*after Guillevic*

Hard rain
then dripping fog
   then snow in your sandals.

Afloat on a blackwater swamp—
cypress knees,
   us feathering oars.

Bats blanket the dark
river, now spiraling
   up the white buildings.

WATER

does that—
assumes the
shape of
other things

even when
attaining a
level all
its own

its beauty
a kind
of trickery

We love
things we
can understand

like water's
filthy green
sky before
a hurricane

MOTE

The mote *is a Spanish form*
of a line or two. Giuseppe
Ungaretti, the Italian
poet, published in 1933
"Mattina" (Morning):

> M'illumino
> d'immenso

He called an earlier draft
"Cielo e mare" (Sky and Sea).

Often a mote *is followed*
by a glosa *or* retruécano
("gloss" or "play on words")
creating a chained form
like a Japanese renga.

*

Here light
shows how

dusting
cleanses

dusting
coats

*

In a mote-
free eye

light is
the floater

breaking sky
from sea

wearing all
the glosses

STILL LIFE

is life
in this
unlit room
that these
cut flowers
instill in
spite of
how dark
it is

and it's
also how
a prairie
still dark
with buffalo
shows life
rising from
a freshly
torched barn

HEINRICH HEINE:
"EARLY ONE MORNING"

She's got my breakfast
Laid on, dark roast
Coffee, double cream,
My loving, lovely wife,

Who pours it out herself,
Joking, flirty, smiling
With lips like nothing
Else in Christendom.

I want to say her voice
Is like a flute. Or,
Like angels. But no—
What do I know of perfect?

She is a perfect beauty.
What should be lily-white
Is. The way that hair should
Frame a face: it does.

Which is why it's odd
This morning to see that she
Could be a bit more slender.
Yes, just a bit slenderer.

VICTOR HUGO: "ECSTASY"

And I heard a mighty voice
     —Book of Revelation

One starry night as I was
watching the waves alone
not a cloud above the sea
without a sail just looking
took me deeper than the world
and tree and mountaintop
the whole of nature seemed to be
murmuring questions randomly
from where the low places surged
to where the high places flamed

and then the stars of gold
their crowns ablaze and waving
in battalions numberless
all spoke in voices loud
or hushed and yet all in
harmony and the blue
surf no force can either
halt or steer spoke also then
nodding its crests of foam
Here is your God, the Lord of Hosts

CHARLES BAUDELAIRE:
"BEAUTY"

Beautiful I am, a very dream of stone.
My perfect torso, where others come to grieve,
Calls out for poets' verses to conceive
A love as timeless and as mute as stone.

Enthroned in the blue, an enigmatic sphinx,
White inside and out, like a swan, like snow,
I still detest, but without a cry or a laugh,
A liveliness that disfigures form's shapeliness.

My grandeur, see, resembles monuments.
So poets, awed by an elevated purpose,
Waste their days away in studiousness.

Even my ardent followers I have blinded by
Allowing them to see what makes things loveliest:
These eyes of mine: mirrors of light eternal.

ECCLESIASTICAL SONNET

His Final Harvest   New Wine   Morning Glory
Open Door   Hope in the City   Door of Hope
Abundant Life   Abiding Love   Greater Peace
Kingdom Seekers   Powertime   Greater Love
City of Refuge   Jubilee Center   PromiseLand
Shepherd of the Hills   Principe de paz
Our Lady of the Angels   Crossroads Praise
Hallelujah Trail   Eternal Way   Victory Center
Wings of Eagles   New Light   Manos de Cristo
Turning Point   Wild Ride   Solid Rock
Sold Out 4 Jesus   Water from the Rock
Church of the Living Water   Cowboy Church
of the Hills   Church of the First Born   Church
of the Friendly Ghost   Floating Outlaw Church

THE 1000 FRAGMENTS

You say I have no new ideas. But the same words,
differently arranged, have different meanings.
As in tennis: both players hit the same ball
but one places it better, with more spin.

Deny a man wine and he won't find truth;
give him too much, the same.

Belief in God is a wise wager.
Winning, you win all;
losing, you lose nothing.

Man's grandeur is knowing himself to be miserable.

—from the work Blaise Pascal
called "The 1000 Fragments"

From his house on Faubourg Saint-Michel,
abutting a garden, between a pair of courts,
the pale geometrician turned theologian
explores the mathematical probabilities
of his belief as he pursues the dream of service.

How good a bet is God? How does tennis
help us reckon His value? Also a wager of faith,
viniculture welcomes the conversion
miracle of the grape—that trick which leaves
a taste of cherry, grass, tobacco, dust.

Which is why grapes terrify, as do
the interstellar darknesses or a drop
shot dying at your feet. That's what we mean
by *terroir*, the arousal of rosé blushes
from white juice, galactic black from red.

*

When unattended by novitiates,
Blaise Pascal practices his backhand,
the torque part, how to check the body's natural
tendency to rotate so that the arm,
straightened, accelerates from the shoulder.

The service, however, is more primal,
an oppositional gesture, the way a man
stays happy in his misery so long
as he denies the Providence he doesn't
know is his already precisely because

he doubts it. To finger the ball, to palm
the racquet, is to bear the cross of winning,
which is thanks to the desire not to lose.
Tossing the ball efficiently high, he applauds
the Lord for his own abjuration of Him.

Isn't this the lack of faith that surprises us
into truth, he muses, thinking himself no better
than a beast trampling the vintage, his mind
a scarecrow warding the warblers off the grapes?
Belief will spare us, he concludes, by how

it breathes into our resistance to it urgings
in the form of words, new, unthinkable ideas
that seem to make the moving ball hover,
hittable now, though we think we aren't yet
close enough to know it. As for the fragments:

real questions require a thousand answers.
When Faith, as it looks through Death, witnesses
one's own fear of it standing across the net,
a wise man, raising his glass, or racquet, bets
on eternity as giving him the better odds

though he may still hit every ball with spin.

3.

STOPPING BY WORDS

A man steps briskly onstage, his shirt out of his pants, mostly. He seems to be headed offstage, then stops, and looks about.

Excuse me.

He turns his back, unbuttons his pants, tucks his shirt in, mostly, turns back around.

OK

Pause

Sorry. My plan was … just to … keep walking. Keep … walking on.

Pause

So.

Pause.

Hello.

Pause.

Is something the matter?

Pause.

????

Short pause

Oh, I see.

Short pause

OK. Let me go first.

Limpid.

It's a word I like, you see. "Lim … pid." I've always liked it. I like that it doesn't mean what it sounds like.
Like you need a cane.
Like when it comes out of your mouth you've got a cold.

Emphatically mouths the word silently.

See how it uses the tongue on the palate, then the lips, then back to the tongue.
Sexy, that.

Pause

Oh boy.

Pause

OK, here's what it is.

Who would you be talking to if you used the word "limpid"?

Pause

OK. I know what you're thinking. When you say "limpid"—
and who doesn't?—you almost always have to tell the person
you're talking to what it means.
Which is the exact opposite of what "limpid" means.
Sure, it's still connected at the hip to "limp." But how to get
from flaccid to limpidity's dazzle of clarity by means of a game
leg is a nifty doesy-doe, lexically speaking.

Not at all limpid.

Which means it's like "pellucid."

You see, don't you? Where I'm going?
Why do you need "pellucid" when a word like "lucid" will
do? What does that little "pel" get you, that Pez-like lozenge
popping out the open mouth of that little lucid cigarette-
lighter-sized candy-popper? Does "pellucid" make "lucid"
more lucid-ic? You know, like the "in" in "inflame" that just
doubles "flame." Like a shirt tucked … in.

Or do we need "pellucid" like a limpid hole in the
inflammatory hole in our head?

Shall I go on?

He starts off, then goes on … talking

You see: it's much like "on." It can mean "forward." The
English mean "on" when they say, "Right mate, I'm off." But
otherwise "on" is a stationary word: "I watched the penguin
on the TV." But is the penguin *on* the TV or on the *TV*? You
see the problem. "On" is stationary but not stable.

Then there's Keats: "Ode *on* a Grecian Urn." But the poem is only *about* the urn, it's not *on* it. Though there *are* things *on* it: pipes and timbrels; heifers; happy, happy boughs; a brede of marble men and maidens overwrought. Like, way overwrought. It's a very busy urn. Not at all pellucid. You get the picture? You could call it a picture poem, a poem about a piece of art.

But then, you get to the end of the poem … a poem about a silent work of art … bride of quietness, etc. … and the urn speaks. Keats has been trying all along to understand how the urn "speaks" to him. But then it just … ups … and speaks. Really speaks.

What it says is: "Beauty is truth, truth beauty."

What the urn says is *in* the poem. The urn, which *is* in the poem that the poem says it is *on*, suddenly says what the urn itself, or for that matter this poem, or for that matter art as such, is all *about*.

You see the problem, for Christ's sake.

Points offstage and starts to move in that direction, as if to say on y va, *which is French, roughly, for* "We're going now." *But he stops.*

You know what's the matter? You know what the matter is? You know who says "on" all the time?

Do you want to know?

I thought so.

Didi and Gogo.

Vladimir and Estragon.

They're characters onstage, in a play, killing time, so to speak, a little bit like the people who go to see them. Like you folks. So they talk. Experiment with words. That's the way they get on with it. One act, it's April (a leaf's on a tree). One act, it's November (the leaf's off it). Thirty days hath, both. Getting on with it, though, and to where, is what they don't know. These boys are waiting. Waiting to … ? No, waiting on … No, waiting for … Waiting about …

Oh, you know.

Fucking prepositions.

And you know what really heats up what they're talking about? The Gospels. How each one of the four—the Gospel guys, I'm talking about—tells a different story even though they're all supposed to say the same thing.

Doesn't this get tiring?

You see, most people want the gospels to tell the story of Jesus, don't they? So, that's why, like Didi and Gogo, they don't like it when there are discrepancies between them.

But that's not what the gospels are about.

They're *on* the subject of Jesus but they're not *about* him.

Pause, as if expecting agreement

OK? So, what *are* they about?

Pause, as if expecting a response

OK, I'll go first.

They're about … Well, they're about …

Pause

They're about … the kind of story … that they're … about.

Now, let's see: this is going to get complicated.

The struggle *of* the gospels is to tell two stories and to tell them *at* the same time—the story of how the Jesus events continue the Scriptures, the *old* law that goes back through David and Moses to Abraham, and also the story of how the Jesus events rewrite and replace the old Scriptures, how they make an entirely *new* law.

But how do you tell the second story without offending those who want the first? How do you tell the first without ignoring what is really new about the second? That's what the gospels are about.

The story of what happens to Jesus? Almost irrelevant.

Unless all you want is reverence, the gospels are really a story about a battle of books.

John, by the way, wins. "In the beginning was the Word, and the Word was God, and the Word was with God." You see what I mean? Point, game, match. Look, he's saying: I'm genuflecting to the old law (in whatever way Jews genuflect), but actually I'm reinventing Genesis. I'm doing it by making Christ, who is the Word, present from the Creation.

Now you see the solution, don't you? If you're not a Jew, that is. And at the end of John's gospel, Thomas says he won't believe *in* Jesus (or what everyone is saying *about* Jesus—that stuff about being resurrected)—unless he can touch the actual wounds *on* Jesus's body.

You remember how all this unfolds. You can almost hear Jesus sighing deeply as he pulls his shirt up: "OK, Thomas, put your finger right in there, into that slit, the one where the sword went. It's still a bit damp, isn't it? A bit crusty, too. Flesh is like that." You can feel Jesus wanting to go on, feel him on a roll, aching to land a rim shot. But then he goes all … um, rabbinical: "Blessed are those," he says, "who have *not* seen and yet believe." He means: blessed are those who believe on the basis of words alone. He means: believe in me—me, the Incarnate Word—because words are all you are going to have to go on, once I vanish. Believe in words, my friends, my disciples, my betrayers: I'm the one metaphor you can bet your life … on.

Pause

OK, sure. I know what you're thinking: there are problems here. Lack of pellucid limpidity.

OK, I'm all tucked in now.

Gesturing towards his trousers, which somehow are ... tucked in

So, just listen.

You'll probably be driving through some traffic on your way home tonight. "Traffic" is *quite* a word. OK, so let's go through it together before you get out there, on the mean streets. "Traffic" entered every European and Near Eastern language at virtually the same historical moment, on or about 1500. In all these languages the word is phonetically almost identical, even in Turkish, which otherwise doesn't resemble any other Western language. And although it means "commerce," is Mediterranean in origin, and is applied specifically to commerce conducted on ships, it always carries the unpleasant overtone of trading in contraband or stolen goods—smuggling, piracy. So, from the start, "traffic" is bad news. But where did the word come from? Why did it materialize suddenly at one time and in one particular place and get spelled pretty much the same in most every language?

Pause

OK, I'll go first.

Early 16th century. Period of vastly expanded shipping and commerce, especially between Europe, or what Europeans were starting to call the West, and what they were now calling the Orient. Linguists, past and present: same prejudices as us. They thought "traffic" sounded vaguely Arabic. It's not, but their ethnic juices got moving in the fast lanes. So to speak. Best current theory? It's a Romany word, the language of the Gypsies—you know, where we get the verb "to gyp," those notorious contraband traders. So, "traffic," a word which stops us from getting home, or just from getting on, is like the word "virtue," the highway onto which we are always seeking to find the right ramp.

But here's the problem with "virtue": The "vir" part in Latin simply means "man." In Anglo-Saxon times, if you killed a man you might have to pay his relatives *wergild*—man-gold or man-wealth—in compensation. Didn't matter if you caused a woman's grief or death. It was about knocking off the guy. *Virtue* is literally manliness.

Let me put it another way. No woman can be virtuous. By definition.

Strange, isn't it? We rarely ever stop for words. Because we are rarely stopped by words, they never really stop us. What we want them to mean means we don't care what *they* want to mean. Let me put this another way. We don't care how words speak, how they speak meanings that we may not want to say, so long as we can put our own meanings *on* them.

There. You see the problem?

Because I just want you to know, you know.

He exits, pulling his shirt all the way out of his pants.

4.

FINDING IT

Without dwelling there:
that's the one way
you'll never lose it.
　　　　—*Tao Te Ching,*
　　　　trans. David Hinton

As my friend
said travel is
one way of
finding other ways
of knowing how
doing without is
what you need
and what you
want is all
you have and
where you've gone
is how you
came first to
know you knew

—*In Memoriam*: Tom Whitbread

LINES WRITTEN UPON REVISITING TINTERN ABBEY AFTER THE SCAFFOLDING HAD BEEN REMOVED

Sheets of bad weather lead to the ruins.
These close at six, as do the ruins.
As do the gift shop and the tea room
Built near the abbey's medieval latrines.
Once the coaches have left with the rain,
However, the pub reopens. Locals pour in.
By seven the sun has begun reflecting
Off the repaired traceries of the great
West window, but less, it seems, remains
Of the two tall east windows, where
Chittering flocks of swallows prey
At evening on the antiquities of the day.

BIRDS OF OZ

Bird calls are not the same as bird songs.
Few Australian birds are actual songsters.

No matter how often,
or when, you descend
on delirious Australia
fair, begirt by several
of the seven seas, you'll
find yourself awaking
in the light that crosses
before dawn, in the hour
of the shining stars,
listening, as you must,
to the grand concertina
of bird-cry sounding

like water as it fills a pipe
like a long wooden match struck in anger
like a steel drummer
like rain in a stand of golden wattle
like your best bud whistling at you from the next corner
like china breaking
no, like stubbies tossed from an Esky onto the shingles
no, like a rocket salad tossed with paw-paw and walnut oil
like the honking of a car, braking
like a recording of many birds singing
like a thrown rod
like water dripping from a pipe
like a pipe being blown through
like a pipe that is not a pipe

like blue hail
like your sister learning to yodel
like a woodpecker working the top of a dead salt cedar
like the devout recoiling from his self-flagellations
like the lies you tell no one but yourself
like an infant crying in the next room
like what one thinks of in the throes of great pain
like what one feels for a long time afterwards

SKYSCRAPERS BY THE SEA

Gold Coast, QLD

There are times when you need
a moon, a full moon, even if
the rising of it is between high-
rises, in the same way you may
need a foaming ebb tide even if
the orange construction cranes
now fronting it are making the foam
seem whiter than white, a comic
rival to the risen moon.

But who needs either surf or moon
anyway, in a poem, when the skyscrapers
leave their own phosphorescence,
having filtered the sun's late fizziness
into eggy slidings of slapstick blue?

THE COLOR OF GUMS

The dry eucalyptus seeks god in the raining cloud.
         —Wallace Stevens, "An Ordinary Evening
         in New Haven"

Their suits are neater abroad,
of denser drape. ...
         —Les Murray, "Eucalypts in Exile"

You are seated in a hardback chair
in a yellow room, feeling
blue, not knowing why,

which is why you start wondering,
could all of this turn, eventually,
green, become a fruitful

wondering, or will it just
go sere, and this is when
you find yourself thinking

of the color of gums
instead, how at a distance
their exhaled terpenoids

will turn distant mountains blue
although seen from a hill across
a pasture they are rows of green

dots, broccoli tops, and yet
walking beneath them, walking
carefully beneath those limbs

called widow-makers, you see
how their sides split, how they
bleed red, yes, but also the color

of diatomaceous earth,
the body paint of Kaurnas
at a corroborree, of shale

slivers, block planings, tailings
of a copper excavation,
chromium-umber corrugations

of tin roofs, flesh-falls
of salmon in cascading foam,
the cinnamon flash of a skate's

wings in the shallows, sidereal
splashings of tuna backs,
spottings of a burnt roux—

blue gum, snow gum, apple
gum, peppermint gum, ghost
gum, a species begun

only after the separation
from Godwanaland, a species
which, when ignited, explodes.

GROUND SONNETS: LATE OCTOBER

As one comes nearer Denver from the air,
before the horizon line turns vertical,
lines appear on the ground which, from the air,
seem random—roads, rivers, trees—al-
though not all. Some come shaped as square
blocks, these blocks following one another
with other lines S-curving inside them—
14-to-a-block, if there's time to count them—
each turning like what the word "verse" meant
once, waiting in turn for what the world calls
snow, which is cloud come to ground, ground
from waves of air into particulates like words,
the way salmon waves of sundown leap over
the cerulean of April, greening Denver.

NORTH OF AUSTIN

When does driving
an Interstate through
central Texas turn
archaeological, the way
the red sediments
of Provence can
turn suddenly sculptural,
a viaduct, say, of
something Gallo-Roman?

(Edging the motorway
are concrete abutments
left from an old
farm-to-market road
still framing the fields
it once passed.)

> So here are
> the lineaments
> of a road, once
> probably dirt,
> that the road you're
> on was built on—
>
> a new thought
> letting out hanks
> of stiff rope
> tries to lasso
> its discovery
> of layeredness …

*

Before Temple is all that's left
in your rearview mirror
the first of hundreds of grain
elevators between here and Muleshoe
lifts off the horizon like a post
we once hitched each horizon to
and then the exit to Troy Auto
Salvage ushers in a host of Waco
off-ramps to Easy Frame Alignments

(one to a Factory Bible Outlet,
all the rest to Hell) and before
long the I-road is U-ing and
Y-ing through the California
incoherence of the Metroplex
a cloverleafage that has left its
cattle brand on every *polis*
in this land which is our land
where Displacedness, true
Avatar of our Country,
plants its lone-starred flag.

And by now you've harmlessly
bypassed the three police forces
of Highland Park and found
the North Central Expressway's
rows of high-rise gold-glassed
office blocks reflecting
(oh say those who still can see)
the reflections off every other

gold-glassed office block
where turkey buzzards rotate
slowly overhead like couples
all aglitter underneath their
honkytonk's mirrored ball.

WHAT I REMEMBER

about peonies is their
tropical largesse
that does not survive
the aridity of Texas
how in full bloom
they fill your palms
with a layeredness
of petals like the genitalia
of a giantess humming
innocently with honeybees
kayaking every fold

and how by late June
the candied air of May
has given way to sprouts
as fisted as Brussels'
the way a theological
debate about grace
may become acts
of humanitarianism
filling the world
with best intentions
but bereft of magic.

WINKELMANN, TEXAS

A Texas highway carnival unfurls again outside Round Top, where a roadside pictograph ↶ turns cars come from Brenham back across four lanes to a past they've just passed through, before a quick right slows them onto, yes, Memory Lane. And what is up there? All you'd expect, perhaps, having gone so far. But if you miss a turn in this cloverleaf rodeo, Shortcut Road offers, a mile on, a wending to where no sign will say.

Off just such a road, Ray Winkelmann dreamed of turning a "here" into a "then," rearranging stilted shotgun houses wrapped by porches and crenelated false-front dilapidations so that they faced one another like settlements that once called out for roads. That was Ray's catch-and-release method of making memories, but farther down the road from his Winkelmann, Texas, now the very ghost town that Ray constructed to resemble one, the Starlite Outdoor Theatre leans, its corrugated tin fencing crusted into the shape of wind, where dark wings flickering against a screen once dimmed fitfully the film's colored lights crisscrossing these spent cotton fields, while inside Dad's car a boy's cupped hand got only as far as a bra before her fingertip traced the U-turn of his ear, for, even then, memories alone were being projected here.

5.

THE EARLY TEXAS SPRING

Only now in
  just February
when even if
  the wind
stills, it still
  burns cheeks,
the world is
  reinventing
pavement again
  as parchment
and birdbaths,
  staying full, tempt
the slow sun
  to empty them.
But can jasmine be
  blooming this soon?
(The empurpling
  of sage will come
in a later,
  wiser flowering.)
Unseen gatherings
  of waxwings
have imprinted
  walk and hood
papyrus-like
  with pulpings
of pyracantha.
  A lone robin
hops toward
  a wall of

scored lime-
   stone pointing
north. Thickets
   of stickweed
or witchgrass
   or whatever we
call it here,
   done with over-
running Bermuda
   and rye, now close
around lacy fronds
   of wild carrot,
choking stands of
   stiff bull thistle.
Meanwhile, buried
   in slopes of lupine
waiting to flower,
   snakes are softening,
skins tightened
   and sloughing down.

FRAGILITY OF SUMMER

Sometimes in July, when my front
lawn is much greener than it is,
usually, in July, I say, almost without
thinking, "How green my lawn is,"
the way at other times I might say
"motherfucker" just to clear my palate,
to wrap my mind around things
or the directions things take
on those days when mint leaves
turn blue beneath an emerald sky.

NEARING THE NEW
YEAR, NEAR BANFF

Dawn starts farther
north of here
quiet like women
whose heads carry
loads too heavy
for their arms

It crosses the
sheer face of
the Wind Tower
taking chips off
the 3 peaks
called The Sisters

It turns on
its side rolling
over once with
a throaty joy-cry
pulling up both
its legs to

the lake side
of the deep
long valley steaming
like breath over
blue snow fields
and loud orange

ice floes like
last summer's noon
when the water
from the tap
singed your hand
it was that cold

JORGE GUILLÉN: "SNOW"

White it lies atop green
And it sings—
Such fine stuff longing to be
Piled high up.

Snow it is that makes the new year glow,
Now green, now white—
Noons are lit by snow which by night
Shines brighter yet.

Specks of powder, flakes of down,
Urgings so compacted—
Snow it is: in your palms
And on your soul.

So unsoiled this passion is, so blanched
And flameless—
Even like blown snow is the snow's song
Rising.

In arbors of snow the new year's lighted.
In ardors of singing.
Lifted mid-song by more snow, the snow,
The snow, is flying. ...

EVERYDAY IMPEDIMENTS

Astronauts aboard the now
officially decommissioned Endeavor
using implements of magnification
most of us can only imagine
were able to see, they tell us, from space
not just the U.S. Air Force Academy,
but its dormitories, not the phallic
uplift of the Washington Monument,
but the sabre-light glinting off it,
a tree's shadow, not just the forest,
not just the standard *invisibilia*
like the dark side of the moon but
the everyday impediments to all
that everyone can see, whether
in orbit or not, and yet they still could not
see how cells eat their own
ability to defend themselves
or how a girl like yours could have
grown into someone who cared
what Andrew would think of her
or why there are no utopian
novels written by women or
how it happened on the way home
on the road that looped around
the pond below the house of the man
in the Norfolk jacket, the pond
you went skating across all winter and
beside which you got laid early
one wet spring, the road you couldn't
now give anyone directions to,
let alone want it to take you
anywhere you'd ever want to be.

OFF-ROAD

No one believes you
can go back and he
went also without
believing the bungalow
he knew would be there
where they lived when
they were so young. ...
When you're so young
you don't believe in
the need ever to go
back anywhere or
so he reasoned out
making that sharp U-
turn off the Boston
Post Road onto
the street dead-ending
into the sea but he
couldn't remember
which of the six
parallel streets it was
all of them being
named for trees and so
the only choice was to
take one after another
turning where each ended
at the sea but missing
their house each time
until he stopped the car
and tried recalling how
they got their mail there
if there was a mailbox

on a post at the street
(none of the streets had
curbs) or was it fixed
beside the front door like
a mezuzah or did they
walk up the street (one of
those he just came down)
often in snow to the top
of the road—ah, is that
he thought why they
call it the Post Road?—
but all he remembered
was how important to him
it was back then how
they got their mail
just as remembering which
dog you had back then
can seem as important
as God sometimes though
why remains a mystery

WALKING HOME,
HAVING DRUNK LATE

But I wasn't,
you know,
drunk, though
before not
much was left
I left. Walking
wasn't unpleasant,
even handy.
I had played
my bad side
off against
my natural
slump to the right
as I often do
at night. And felt
all right, not
queasy, you know,
not in that
starboard, meditative
posture of resignation
it's easy to effect.
This feeling
all right
went on, along
with its effects,
making my way
eye out for rocks.
Which is when
I noticed
stars.

So this is it
I thought.
A trillion light-years.
The night got chilly.
I noticed that.
Then all was
as it ever is.

SNOW-BOUND

Flat light: in winter when the air is clear and there is little or no snow falling, and yet the ground is completely snow covered, diffuse or "slant" light from overcast clouds may cause all surface definition to disappear. "Shadows hold their breath," in Dickinson's words. It becomes difficult to measure distances.

Looking out
in Massachusetts
at the flat
light Emily
called a "slant"

smoking a pipe
and thinking,
is this like
Baudelaire's
pipe d'auteur … ?

Call it four
o'clock. Call
it February.
A few degrees
above or below.

Shadows
eaten up
by ground snow.
Myself
eaten up also,

afternoons
like those,
by what I have
long since
lost track of.

APNEA

It's not that you just miss
something, it's the condition
of missing something as
a condition of being
albeit less than functional
everything a bit delayed
holding its breath as it were
while the beauty of sleep
grinds its full-load down-
shifting eighteen-wheeler
past you and so no wonder
sweet jesus you refuse to
exhale when everything before
you sets your teeth on edge

THE CHROMATIC SCALE
BETWEEN JOY AND SORROW

When you make yourself mad
thanks to something you've done,
you may turn to poetry, may
write some of your own, even,
which could get quite loud
like the trapezing of those wrens
on the clothes line, or like the way
after a heavy spring rain so
many cool lilies of the invisible
may for two, or even three,
days flower sufficiently to make
you forget for maybe a day, maybe
two, the stupidities you own,
the raw scars you still pick at
while you keep on trying to
hear how calm, how dour
those warblers at the grapes are.

6.

AUGUST KOPISCH:
"THE HEINZELMÄNNCHEN"

Ripe in those days was old Cologne
For the advent of the Heinzelmännchen.
For when people were tired, or lazy back then,
They just took it easy, reclined, packed it in.
  Under cover of night
  These little folk swarmed
  Clapped and banged
  Plucked and tugged
  Hopped and trotted
  Scraped and scrubbed
And by the early light of the next dawn
The new day's work ... was already done.

In the midst of their shavings ankle-deep
The carpenters stretched out and took a kip.
The Heinzelmännchen meanwhile slipped in
To finish up what these workers slept off.
  With ax and adze
  And froe and wedge
  They chiseled and sawed
  And whacked and stacked
  Mortised and tenoned
  And left the beams
Joisted and upright and just like that
The entire house was ... trussed and done.

Bread at the bakery was abundant—
The Heinzelmännchen baked it—
For when the apprentices lay down
The Heinzelmännchen rose up
   Groaning and moaning
   Under the heavy sacks
   They kneaded and tapped
   And weighed precisely
   Flattened and swept
   And shoved and poked
While all the boys snored in choral union
Until the bread emerged … in hot fresh buns.

A similar life the butcher led.
While the apprentices lay in bed
The Heinzelmännchen learned
To cleave the hogs from stem to stern.
   As quick as a mill
   They rinsed and culled
   Honed and wiped
   Skewered and carved
   Stirred and mixed
   And finally stuffed
Until the apprentices awoke to smell
Rows of sausage dangling for them to sell.

At the vintner, too, it went like this:
The cooper drank until he finally sank
Dead asleep across the pipes and casks.
Out from the butts and churns and tubs
       The Heinzelmännchen
       Rolled and lifted
       Sulphurized barrels
       Winched and swiveled
       Blended and poured
       And in the end stored
All the while the cooper snored
The wine that they had corked and waxed.

At the tailor's shop was left the Mayor's coat
With this note: Make sure it's done today.
But in the face of this rush he tossed
His tools off, left his stool, and snoozed.
       The little ones laid out
       The table's full length
       And scissored and brushed
       And sewed and stretched
       Embroidered and hemmed
       Trimmed and stroked
And when the master arose at four
The Mayor's coat was fitted … and hung up there.

But the tailor's wife had a sneaky suspicion—
Neighbors even thought her a stinky magician.
So, the next night, though it came as a big surprise
The little ones found her stairs strewn with peas
      And their feet slipped
      Landing head-first
      Their eyes rolled
      Their ears wagged
      From their tongues shot
      A few raw shouts
Until she ran from her room with a torch and a broom
But poof—nothing was there to be seen … but peas.

So? Is even one Heinzelmännchen left here
In Cologne? No, they have all disappeared.
No one takes now his daily rest as before.
What faces them now is work they shunned before.
      Tired or not
      All must lift
      Themselves up
      Prod themselves
      To stitch and nail
      Simmer and stir
For the days of yore are no more. The whole town yearns
For them but the Heinzelmännchen will never return.

7.

IN THE SAME YEAR

In the same year I was born
Marianne Moore's mother died.
Some think the mother, Mary,
helped Marianne write
some of her poems. Or at least
research and edit them. We
know they slept in the same bed.
The gravestone her daughter
made for her left lines for
Marianne herself, her dates
and those of her husband
should she have one. Mary
was sixty years old. Over sixty
myself now, I am missing,
I think, Marianne most,
the one who first danced so
close to me I couldn't breathe,
or what I was breathing was
her self breathing me, almost
like kissing. Don't get me
wrong. We never kissed. Or
anything. Some years on—we'd
lost touch—she killed herself.
No one knew why. Marianne
Moore went on to write her
singular poems no one ever
thought personal. I write mine.

AFTERWARDS

Reading it just now I knew
they had started, the slippages
one must learn to expect,

those common places
it is commonplace
not to place too precisely.

What I read about
was you. That you'd died.
What I remembered, then,

was how surrounded we'd been
by all those ducks, the green
air faintly fair but failing,

as we talked of how many
vectors lives at twenty could
take, how joy shakes so

many hands before going
indoors. We were tossing
crumbs onto the redolent grass

and into the smoking lake.
You spoke of how the unexpected
pregnancy possessed you

with alarming liquidities,
of how you loved him and
would join him after finals,

and yet you seemed to be tossing
in the air wine glasses that never
landed on any floor you'd walk

barefoot across for the rest
of your life. That's how
you put it back then, your voice

grasping the gunwales
of your next half-century
for which we had become

odd spectators, you and I,
two old people who don't stop
speaking just because someone

else is speaking, and so we
ended up kissing. Not
the kind of kissing one

kisses so as not to
talk any more, hoping for
something more, but

only to stop talking. Up, then—
but it happened so much later—
from that duck-muddle

arose this new sense:
just because something happens
doesn't make it true, only real.

READING THE CLOCK

Some time after
I learned to tell time
from the clock face

I asked my father
how old I would be
in the year 2000

Let's sit down he said
in the voice he used to
teach me how
to read a clock

or the rules of golf
and do the math

In the year 2000
he would be
ninety-three

and he made it
nearly

By then
I knew more about
bodily decrepitude

without a stroke
of cognitive
impairment

In the year 2000
I published a book

of poetry
my first

At the time
it seemed like
something

like telling time
or breaking 90

Then it didn't

RYKER'S REVEILLE

Wake up he said it's morning time.
He went to ask his mother what time
it was, sent by his mother's mother
Amu who was in sleep-time still.
Ten to eight he returned in no time.
Are you sure asked Amu that that's
the time. He went to ask his mother
what that was again. What what was
she asked. He said again what that time
was. Ten past eight she said and that
was what that time was he said again
coming back to tell his Amu this time.

THE WARMTH OF WINTER

Wallace Stevens is on a train now,
                          in its foremost Pullman,
taking him to St. Paul,
                 that frozen river city, the one
that one must cross
                 the river of rivers to enter.
He has just placed a round jar
                          of bootleg back into his valise,
picked up on the stopover in Chicago.

This train will not be stopping tonight
                          in Clinton or Shopiere
or anywhere else
                 the rail lines have begun bypassing forever.
And by the time the train has reached the area
                 called Driftless, bypassed by glaciers,
Wallace Stevens,
           surety attorney, will be asleep.

In the rheumy winter dusk
                 my father hasn't finished milking yet.
The oil lamps swing in the crisp breeze
                 passing through the cracks in the timbers
and freshening the barn a bit
                          for electricity will not
light this part of rural America
                 for another decade, another fact
of life to check against
                 its prologues to what is possible.

My father has spent the last warmth
                              of this winter afternoon
in the spring house
                    mending tackle, because here
the temperature is always like
                              the early Wisconsin spring
and so his gloves are off
                         as he makes the harness leather
answer to the pull of stitch, the ebullience of lanolin
                              that keeps the skin
of his hands smooth and limber
                                   seventy-five years later
even when it's become parchment-thin.

He walks from milking now
                         toward the house of darkened windows
past snowfields glowering around him
                                   like a stage-set
backlit, as it were,
                    by the faint overhead Aurora.
He is not yet afraid
                    of global depression and war, genocide, renal failure—
the real theatre of the century he will live the fullness of.
Perhaps he pictures a son
                         listening after all the lights
have failed
            to a train passing
like the one whose horn
                       my father has lifted his head, just now, to hear.

8.

A VALEDICTORY ADDRESS

IN MEMORY OF THE BIRTHDAY PARTY

FOR ST. IGNATIUS

Bread Loaf, Vermont
School of English
Summer 1972

In what history now calls a "summer of blood," to party at all
    took finesse, real finesse—call it
    our backdoor miracle. We
    spread our loaves with fishes—

sockeye or tuna (sometimes Spam)—and laced our rum with the real,
    the classic Coke (though all
    original spirits in it had been
    long since de-coked).

One night the Jesuits threw two birthday parties for their patron saint,
    Ignatius, but the one where we
    would drink till dawn came after
    the Mass, and this left us,

Fra Sidney from Queens stepped forth to confess, "no wine to drink."
    Which was not exactly true,
    however unalterably correct.
    Jugs of it there were, courtesy of

the Brothers Gallo and Almaden (that lost brand), but not a drop of it
     potable, the wine being blooded still
     by the Fathers' prior consecration,
     now neither trope nor nature.

Some called it unusually, almost rabbinically, tough luck
     there in those after-hours
     when someone walking off
     a mountaintop, hoping to have

counted the streaks of an evening's Perseid shower, could run
     into a Loyolan conundrum
     pitting *desideratum* against
     fortuna, the starfall

you wanted versus the moonball you got. But can sacrilege
     be committed by mistake,
     the way a random oyster may
     fox even an abstemious liver?

Could a priest bless something—anything—by accident?
     So it was that the stout Fathers
     argued their case, slaloming
     between host and guest, balancing

the ripe pineapple of doctrine against the dull machete of grace,
     pressing the needle's eye of dogma
     into stricter crosshairs, friendlier
     fire, until the jungle-green

mountaintops of Vermont heard the voice of the law
        melt into garnets of pinot
        noir, carnelians of cabernet,
        fire opals of cool rosé,

by dint of a breath-test, *o mio Sid*, worthy of the holiest.

                    *   *   *

Right then, of course, ladies and gentlemen, I knew I'd be
        a teacher. I remembered a poster
        I found one teenaged afternoon
        in England one bloodless summer.

I was standing at the porch of a forgettable Norman church,
        its axis not merely off-line (for,
        as you know, they all are) but
        quite wrong. I was there because

deciphering ancient gravestones in the rain had left me
        counting up all the girls I
        would never date back home.
        Beside the 16th-century

double-doors, a bulletin board announced our century's stuff:
        child-care hours, evensong,
        a bring-and-buy sale, rewards
        for lost Shelties. And there it was,

much faded—a French chef's knife beside a sliced loaf,
       goblets of claret, black as Guinness,
       in the block-print of a ransom note:
       YOU ARE ALL INVITED TO MY HOUSE.

Call what I felt then hunger if you call paychecks satisfaction.
       A *longueur*—or was it
       just being soaked through
       all that summer?—made a backdoor

in the labyrinth of this declaration open into an exclamation.
       Where faith means to leap
       without finesse. Where to eat
       means the taste of body,

a tongue of blood. Where to enter is to go all the way in.

          *   *   *

At Bread Loaf the faith of the Fathers left them only one
       recourse which, students of piety,
       they took: the profane joy of company.
       While we gossiped they unseated

from their ancient vows the benedictive stuff that leaves
       to human imbibers its sulfites
       esters, cream of tartar, tannin
       (oxidized), and unconverted sugar,

elevating their triglycerides but leaving the transubstantial
        untrespassed. And this is where,
        as you've learned, we can hear
        the gears of Reformation grinding

the magic of human sacrifice into the efficacy of prayer,
        which is internal and voluntary,
        converting flagellated desire
        into situational ethics.

Take my son, for instance, who is fretting out, one room
        away, Bach's first suite for
        cello, following Pablo first,
        then Yo-Yo, two tapes,

and fighting the beginner's wish to keep the left hand in
        first position, even as the long
        line longs for a bow-work
        so intricate in the right. …

And now I think I may have been mistaken this whole while.
        (Note here the valedictorian's
        backdoor miracle: confession.)
        I may have made too much

of what was, like providence itself, merely a local adjustment
        for historical accident.
        Nor am I sure that Father
        Sid wasn't really Brother Dan

or some Paul or other from Sioux Falls. Nor can I recall
    (my worst failing here)
    the name of my best friend
    from that summer, a novitiate

who retreated that very weekend to a hotel in Montpelier
    to decide whether, then how,
    to get laid. Some years later,
    I learned, on the Lincoln corner

of the lane which joins the Turl and Camera, he used a paving
    stone against his own skull
    after the woman he'd left
    the Order for sent him her

four-line Dear-John letter, written both in blood and Latin.
    He ingested old Father Hopkins
    (of course), gorged himself on Joyce,
    and was drinking hard

to dodge the draft (first on, then to spite, the wings of the church).
    And so we lost touch. (I've
    lost even his name.) Why
    did I believe he had died?

When did I start seeing him, as today, seated there among you?

THE DANCER'S INTERVIEW

for Tishani Doshi

Her left palm crosses
as a question
alights atop her right
shoulder

Her torso verses
left
then reverses

Her feet crossed
under the table
lift slightly
like a struck match
before coming to
rest again

At once her fingers
flicker overhead
as if netting raindrops
and a songbird flashes
like a ring
past her ear
while a silent
iridescent hummer
no larger than her little finger
hovers
where her mouth is
now in flower

TOEING THE LINE
LIKE MASON AND DIXON'S

She taught you how
poetry happens
in the mouth

how the name
of a sound
is not the sound
of the sound

"Happy"
is not
the same
p *as*
"promise"

She warned you
how QWERTY
might keep you
from touching

her intimate folds
her little tower

or from naming
her favorite composers
Rimsky-Korsakov
Dominick Argento
with your palate and tongue

If there were birds outside
you couldn't name

with a whistling
that ended in gargling

you are not to
kill she said
any mockingbird
even if it grackles

When she called you
Lovebird
her lips met
and parted

carefully

And then she brought you
to a kind of Natchez Trace

a ripple creasing
the Deep South
of your stomach

that made you long
to pull over
and eat with her

at Birmingham
and Macon

because everywhere else
you went
there was only hunger

THE ONE WITH THE LONG NOSE

All bull behind the screen, she paws
the red shag redder, snorting, ready
to rip through the mesh if I'm
not fast enough, then beelines it
to the base of our six-foot cedar fence,
snapping and growling, slaloming
between it and the oleanders
lining this side of it, to tell off
those creatures on the other side,
whose yapping has ruined
most of the morning—then shits,
kicks dirt, comma-curling her long
back for the leap to our back
step—a slo-mo hyperbola
of dachshund hyperbole—
and, alighting there, yawns. …

*   *   *

I examine her closely, through the screen,
before letting her in. At war's end,
forces advancing from our side
found those from the other side,
some with the same names as ours,
wandering wordless, incontinent,
having eaten their dachshunds,
for they had no food.

*   *   *

Homer's heroes
         fed their dogs,

                      mongrels who gathered

where war was,
         the severed

                      genitalia of the slain.

*   *   *

A strip of sunlight
splits the hall in two,
her sleek black body
Maltese-Crosses it.
The strip of sunlight
splits again and then
she's part Mondrian.
On a chaise longue,
paw on my curled hand,
she nestles the dry weight
of her long jaw into
the taut V of my groin.

*   *   *

The toddler wakes this morning
on her tongue her double name
daw daw for the long nosed one
who has crawled under her crib.
When I come in to take her out
she barks *da da no* and then
mummy mummy and burrows
into the three-point stance—
knee, knee, and knucklebone—
of newborns and weak-side
noseguards, until sleep pins her
wet cheek to the mat again.

*   *   *

Waking this morning
to crow-flap and the low
flak of careening gulls
I hear no dogs barking

but to my side
past a row of pillows
the one with the long nose
is the only one snoring.

THREADS OF THE ARGUMENT

Let us take up the thread of the argument
which has led us to where we now are:
let us extend our first assumption.
                    —A. R. J. Turgot

I take up what you alone
have power to extend. Of course you think
I'm joking. (My penchant, you might say,
for overstatement.)
But how will we ever
take ourselves seriously
if someone who is always piping in
Where do armadillos come from?
pipes in again.
And that was after
you had put him to bed a third time,
who returned, armed with curiosity
gratified as I was
leaning determinedly against you, talking
behind a door closed against the lights left on.
Someone only just eight years old,
bursting through doors
that won't lock
even if we wanted them to,
into rooms that we dare not darken,
calls out
for aeonian patience,
the work of glaciers.

\#

What a sentence you came up with!

Again we started
tying together
the threads of our argument
when a quick, politic knock on the door
precedes a timely return to native soil
(like the voice-over of Chamberlain in the old newsreels:
I have in my hand a piece of paper ...).

All right, then.
                    We give it up
agreeing
          informally
to get back to each other
                      later.

#

A message is always sequential:
it's that variation in a series of repetitions
which makes a difference
is what you said, more or less, in due course.
But try
telling that to a dachshund
who is wagging his tail underfoot
after having gone off and done *that* again,
or to the child
toweling off his penis
after his bath, after you clearly informed him
it was absolutely now
now now now
now time for bed.

\#

Yellow roses open in a blue vase
atop a television set, at last turned off.
There is mud on the bathroom floor.
Those who can't say *I have to pee*
won't wait out seriality, as when
you say *Why don't you*
deal with the dog tonight
followed by *Who will tuck in the boy?*
spoken *by* the boy, the only
one among us, evidently,
who can take a bath alone.
O Chamberlain!
And what of poor Turgot—
all that scholarly passion for fine detail
in the face of all those things that wouldn't wait
to be gone into,
chanting
no taxes, no bankruptcy, no borrowing
until the king had no choice
but to axe him.

#

Like Hansel and Gretel making their way
home through the woods, having found a way,
in spite of themselves, of getting lost again,
we lie in bed
around 2 A.M.
listening to a bird singing. Could I name it, you ask,
knowing I can. Tomorrow, you remind me
(which is, of course, today),
is somebody's birthday
you knew I'd forget.
Admitting nothing, I concede everything,
the argument endlessly extended
from assumptions relentlessly agreed to.
Lying on one side, you take me back
to my first one, a bit distended now,
more memorial than marmoreal.
Can you make me you whisper
over your turned cascading shoulder *a poem
that goes something like this.*

ABOUT THE AUTHOR

A native of Wisconsin, Kurt Heinzelman lived for a number of years in western Massachusetts. His work as a poet, scholar, and translator is widely published. He is also an editor, having co-founded two literary journals, *The Poetry Miscellany* and *Bat City Review*, and served as editor-in-chief of *Texas Studies in Literature and Language*. He lives in Austin, Texas where he is Professor of Poetry and Poetics at the University of Texas and is a faculty member in the Michener Center for Writers.

Here are some comments about his previous books of poetry:

"In *Intimacies & Other Devices* Kurt Heinzelman has created a marvelous *hommage* to the erotic in all its forms and manifestations, a world in which, as he so originally puts it, taste's 'one true *sommelier*' is beauty. ... A wonderful book, one that will bring pleasure, in the deepest sense, to all who encounter it."
—Michael Blumenthal

"It is wonderful to experience a poet's bounty ..., to participate in the playful re-interpretation of long traditions in the hands of one who knows, to feel the spring of poetic rhythm and the eloquence of the intricately concentrated expression, as memory, desire, humor and sensuality are shaped in virtuosic language."
—Nicholas Jose

"Heinzelman's ... collection is ... replete both with intimacies and with the great range of devices poets and lovers employ. ... [T]hese poems are wildly imaginative and very, very sexy."
—Ellen Doré Watson

"In *The Names They Found There* Heinzelman creates a poetry of place with an unerring eye and ear for the ways that landscape can be mapped in the twists and turns of language. As in his previous wonderful book, *The Halfway Tree*, he displays, in equal parts, a

128

mastery of sight, sound, and intellection."
—Michael Davidson

"*The Names They Found There* travels from Pflugerville to Wellfleet, Australia to Istanbul. Its poems, populated by Ben Franklin and Jacobus Vrel, Sonny Rollins and Warren Spahn, speak of flying foxes and fricatives, baseball and *pêches jaunes*, sweet corn and Incan *quipus* and 'capless Bics in a Styrofoam cup' at a taco kiosk on concrete blocks. 'And what of all this / luminous / curiosity,' one of Heinzelman's poems asks. ... [T]he question can be answered in musical terms: Heinzelman's curiosity is luminous, yes, but also canorous, 'A continuo of / the familiar, ... under which / discontinuities / of the exotic.'"
—H. L. Hix

"These poems artfully negotiate what we know by name and what we know by heart. These poems travel; each 'road spills / its cargo of hooks.' What a thrill to discover this etymology of place, of self."
—Susan B. A. Somers-Willett

"Heinzelman commands 'any stroke of available light' to deliver luminous concoctions of history, music, and heart. A beautiful smart book."
—Barbara Ras

"At a time when so many poets whittle themselves down into defining personal styles and subjects—into what the Polish poet Adam Zagajewski has dubbed 'deft miniaturists of a single theme'—Kurt Heinzelman writes a restless, free-ranging poetry, rarely repeating a form or approach. In a Heinzelman book, you're likely to encounter ballads, Pindaric odes, sonnets, ekphrastic poems, short lyrics, one-sentence poems, and long, elastic sequences, all handled with remarkable skill and ease."
—Brian Barker

CPSIA information can be obtained
at www.ICGtesting.com
Printed in the USA
FFOW03n0128311017
41716FF